# THE
# FAT MAN

# THE FAT MAN

## SELECTED POEMS
## 1962~1972

# JOHN NEWLOVE

McCLELLAND AND STEWART

ISBN: 0-7710-6733-X


McClelland and Stewart Limited
*The Canadian Publishers*
25 Hollinger Road, Toronto


Printed and bound in Canada

CANADIAN CATALOGUING IN PUBLICATION DATA

Newlove, John, 1938—
   The fat man

ISBN 0-7710-6733-X

I. Title.

PS8527.E94F38    C811'.5'4    C77-001337-6
PR9199.3.N4F38

*To F. R. Scott*

**BOOKS BY JOHN NEWLOVE**

Grave Sirs (1962)
Elephants, Mothers & Others (1963)
Moving in Alone (1965)
Notebook Pages (1966)
What They Say (1967)
Black Night Window (1968)
The Cave (1970)
Lies (1972)


Editor:
Canadian Poetry: The Modern Era (1977)

Nun bin ich beinah 40 Jahre
und habe eine kleine Versfabrik.

—Erich Kastner


This story is comical and strange,
but it is a little dreadful also.

—Silvia Risolo,
letter to the London *Times*, 29/6/49

**CONTENTS**

**NOTE**
A number of the poems have been revised.

from *Elephants, Mothers & Others*

**THE ARRIVAL**

Having come slowly, hesitantly
at first, as a poem comes,
and then steadily down to the marshy seaboard:

that day I ran along the stone sea-break,
plunging into the Pacific, the sun
just setting, clothed, exuberant, hot,
so happy—
        o sing!
plunging into the ocean, rolled on my back, eyes
full of salt water, hair in eyes,
shoes lost forever at the bottom, noting
as if they were trivia
the wheeling birds of the air
and gulls gorging themselves
on the sea-going garbage
of civilization, the lower mainland,
hauled away by tugs—
        they,
being too heavy to fly,
and foolish-looking there,
can be knocked off with sticks
from barge into ocean—

and noting the trees whitely flowering,
took off my clothes and calmly bathed.

## MY DADDY DROWNED

My daddy drowned still blind kittens
in the rainbarrel corner of our white house
& I make poems babies & love-affairs
out of women I've only seen once

or maybe never at all. Daddy
had to push those kittens under in a sack *(bed )*
to keep them from squealing & I don't know
whether he hated or enjoyed it; no expression

was permitted to cross his legal face. I'm
the same way, Freud says so, I let
no expression on my lips when I read,

*domination*pushing those women underneath
to drown in poems. It's one way
to get them down. But I wonder about daddy,
if he's the same as me,
                              because sometimes
I let those women slip to the surface
& squeak a little bit before I kill them.

## BEFORE THE BIG BEND HIGHWAY

I stand on the west corner of that road
(going the opposite way this time)
outside Revelstoke, watching the hoods
drive back and forth, dangerously,
the same oiled quartets each time,
eyeing and laughing: I consider the night
just passed, spent nearly in rain,
partly in cold and windy showers before
the downpour, then how the rest of it
went in the dark cabin
                    of that mad old man,
flopped on the wooden floor,
deliciously at his insistence
reading Ezekiel to him, Ezekiel
whom he loved, Ezekiel who prophesied,
he said, The End Of The World,
deeply rolling the rhetorical syllables,
the allegory of Gog . . . .

**NOT MOVING**

Waterfalls
in the dark
& the noise

very much

    the animals
    undoubtedly
    moving there
    & waiting

rocks
rolling down
the gravel
cuts
of the road

    there
    bears be
    pack rats (curious
    to see (snakes
    lizards

deer moving
among
the trees
quietly

also
on the side
of the road
me

    smoking
    nervously
    at midnight
    100 miles
    to go

& cold
& afraid
on the side of the road

the only animal

    not moving
    at all.

## VERIGIN

The pure white bodies of my friends,
d'un blanc pur, like—
like a cigarette paper ! shivering

in cold spring before a cold
shallow waterhole. Thin naked
bodies, ribs, knees, buttocks, hearts,

young bilingual doukhobors,
where are you now? I cut my foot
on a piece of rusty tin and walked
home alone, shoe full of blood.

## WHITE CAT

I like orange juice
better than anything else
in the world, she said—
wearing a blue dress;

when I wrote it down,
drinking cold tapwater she
turned and, What
did you do? said, then

came, sat in
the rocker chair, picked
up the small white cat,
said, This cat is

sick, John, do you think
she has distemper? And
when I said, How should
I know, she touched

the cat again, held it
up, regarding the eye
it had injured weeks earlier,
said, Is it? Is it?

**ELEPHANTS**

aren't any more important
than insects,

but I'm on the side
of elephants,

unless one of them tries
to crawl up my leg!

from *Moving in Alone*

## WITH WHOM SHOULD I ASSOCIATE?

With whom should I associate
but suffering men? For all men
who desire suffer; and my desires
are too great for me to hold to
alone. I must see the others,
hear them in their plans, console
and ridicule, knowing
the greater their desires
the more they understand of me.

**FOR JUDITH,**
**NOW ABOUT TEN YEARS OLD**          1O

Judith, niece, red
welted scars on
your not yet
adolescent chest,

slits cut, say,
yearly, so you
may lift your arms,

welt ridges also
on the not even yet
about to be

womanly posterior
from where
the failing grafts
were taken, girl

who pulled down
on your birthday, I
think I remember,

the scalding water
from the black,
polished, wood-burning
stove, screaming,

so young, perhaps
10 ten now, years after,
do you remember
the prairie town

you were ruined in,
can you recall
the smell of it,

the smell you had?
What will you do
when your breasts come?

I don't know. I remember
the feel of your tough
rubber-laced skin
as I spread salve on it.


Moving in Alone, 1965

## FOUR SMALL SCARS

This scar beneath my lip
is symbol of a friend's rough love
though some would call it anger,
mistakenly. This scar

crescent on my wrist
is symbol of a woman's delicate anger
though some would call it love,
mistakenly. My belly's scar

is symbol of a surgical precision:
no anger, no love. The small
fading mark on my hand

is token of my imprecision,
of my own carving, my anger and my love.

**THE FLOWERS** *outside* (for my brother)          *in italics*

It is raining, rain
streaks down the window to my left,
cars sluice water in the gutters
in the night, the round
neon clock-containing sign
hanging outside beside my window
sways in the wind and buzzes.

The flowers sprout everywhere,
in pots and boxes, on lawns
and trees, in gardens and ditches
the flowers are growing; the wet
wind will nourish them, cut
some down but feed the rest.

The sign crackles
and swings on its bar,
iron bar; the cars go by
all the night. They cut
a momentary trail and mark,
disappearing, on the wet
black pavement. The cars go by,
the police in their cars
prowl restlessly
up and down the rainy avenue
looking for interlopers, anyone
afoot at night in the rain,
the blue and dangerous
gun-hipped cops.

The car came smashing
and wrecking his face, his head,
poor hit hurt head
bleeding on the roadway
and in the cool hospital
night in bandages
and glued-on tape.

His eyes, they said,
were soft and easy
years ago. Now
he wears them cleverly
like some secret
coupled badge,
twin and original, dark
ice eyes that watch and assess
slowly what they have
fixed
on; his head does not move.

In the hospitals
with antiseptic nurses
stripping him, knife-
fisted surgeons bending down,

they cut, irony,
to save his life; and he stayed
days and years filled
with tantalizing drugs, interminable
dreams, tangled in bandages and
shocks, suspicions, a nonchalant
profusion of hopes and cures,
surrounded by the tears
of his rainy crazy peers.

Rain, wind, and spring, all things
drove him crazy and grow
flowers, flowers
that dance in the rain,                    ————— stanza break
the bulging flowers that grew
in his head, plants
of evil or god, some
holy epileptic angel, bloated
inhuman flowers shining
their bright colours
insistently, turning
slowly in the wind
and spring, tortuous
creaking growths, thick
cancerous things
in the rain, stems
like the barrels of rifles,     *muzzles*
fat lead bullet roots
gripping the damp earth.

And the cars
pass up and down
the streets, disappearing
trails, the blue police
pass, coughing *delicately*
behind their leathery fists,
guns dangling
from their hips, eyes
watching. My flowery clock
buzzes and mutters,
typewriter taps
like the rain. I breathe
as harshly as the wind.

*Moving in Alone, 1965, 1977*

25

## THE SINGING HEAD

The singing head that
does not falter when
it falls

but sings for seven
short years more, or nine,

or for as long
as it may be lucky
to shout out the words
in measured time

or to the ear's delight
to hear

the auditory
nerves carry on
the sound,

the self-made sound
the mouth manufactured

of the air,
of the endless
chant of praised delight

that could
not feel the sword or
cry to feel its hot
blood gush

where the neck had led
to the carolling lungs
and balanced body tilting

in the wind, the head
in grass or just

tossed under any bush
or muddled in a ditch . . .

it carries on
to raise its breathless voice,
to praise

the life that while it lived
was good, to praise
the grass
or bush or muddy ditch,

that where it stays
is good.

**EAST FROM THE MOUNTAINS**

The single, faltering, tenuous line of melody
displayed by a thin man's lungs
unsurely, halting in the winter air:

what to say? Oh, say nothing.
But listen to the blowing snow
at the house's wooden corner,
listen to the misery in the sound of the wind.

On a single wind, followed
by lonely silence, the snow
goes by. Outside
everything is gone; the white
sheer land answers no questions,
but only exists

as it ought to, the sun
shines now as it ought to shine,
shedding no warmth:
what to say.

To listen to the high-pitched wind
in winter removes the idea of hills,
makes clear the real geometry
of the land: east from the mountains
and east to the giant lakes and the river
no single distinction to ruin
the total wholeness of sweep
of the earth, untouched by the lights
of the cold and isolate cities:

following the tentative line
of a gully, it becomes lost at last
as in Qu'Appelle; following
the tentative line of the railway,
it gathers together and disappears;
the perspective is textbook,
the rare protuberance never in mind.

The cities do not extend to each other,
the hamlets exist alone,
the suspicious basses of voices
of farmers mutter in the horse-
urined yards, the wives and the children
wait for the spring, summer, fall, the grass,
the quick, unlasting reprieve, gone

like that!—and so hard
to hear what someone is saying:
it is important and real, what is said,
in the thrown-together town,
but is heard from a long way away,
hollow or shrill, and heard
with trouble. So hard

to attend as the issuing words
emerge from an icy tunnel of lung,
faltering, tenuous melody—

o tired and halting song!

## THE WELL-TRAVELLED ROADWAY

The dead beast, turned up
(brown fur on back and white
on the belly), lay on the roadway,
its paws extended in the air.

It was beautiful on the well-travelled roadway
with its dead black lips: God help me,
I did not even know what it was.
I had been walking into the city then,
early, with my own name in mind.

## TWO LETTERS FROM AUSTRIA

Out of any thing at hand, once
out of three hungry days
in the bush, spider-devilled and scared,
trotting down the woodsy roads at midnight,
woods dreamed full of bears
as Granville Street with cops, even the deer
dangerous, wrapped in death; once
out of a single glass of cider,
other things numerously crowding in,
poems are begun. And now
a pair of letters, not even new,
from a barely-known girl in Austria.

You say, serious girl, Sorry for this weak
green effort. But names of places
are three feet deep in these letters, made
real by your excited presence in them;
these things form poems when I allow it.

Oh no, I'm not in love with you, or will be.
It's too easy to fall in love by letter,
at long distance too many things
may be ignored. But your letters
make me real in one more mind and make places
briefly more real for me. I can fill up poems
with them. And since
you are smarter than I am and know
this act of writing is an act of love,
although you do not love me either,
you sign your letters: Love.     ( ; is , )

_Moving in Alone_, 1965, 72

31

## VERIGIN, MOVING IN ALONE

fatherless, 250 people
counting dogs and gophers
we would say, Jmaeff's grocerystore,
me in grade 4, mother
principal of the 2-building
3-room 12-grade school,

a boy sitting on the grass
of a small hill, the hot fall,
speaking no russian, an airgun
my sister gave me making me envied.

I tried all fall, all spring
the next ominous year, to kill
a crow with it, secretly glad
I could not, the men
in winter shooting the town's
wild dogs, casually tossing
the quick-frozen, barely-bleeding
head-shot corpses onto
the street-side snowbanks,

the highway crews cutting their way
through to open the road with what
I was sure was simply
some alternate of a golden summer's
wheat-threshing machine, children
running through the hard-tossed spray,
pretending war from the monster's snout,

leaping into snowbanks
from Peter The Lordly Verigin's
palace on the edge of town
in a wild 3-dimensional
cubistic game of cops and robbers,

cold spring swimming
in Dead Horse Creek and farmers' dugouts
and doomed fishing
in beastless ponds, strapped
in school for watching a fight,

coldly holding back tears
and digging for drunken father's
rum-bottle, he had finally
arrived, how I loved him,
loved him, love him, dead, still.

My mad brother chased me
alone in the house with him
around and around
the small living room, airgun,
rifle in hand, silently
our breaths coming together—

all sights and temperatures
and remembrances,
as a lost gull screams now
outside my window,
a 9-year-old's year-long
night and day in tiny
magnificent prairie Verigin:

the long grey cat we got,
the bruised knees, cut fingers,
nails in feet, far walks
to watch a horse's corpse
turn slowly and sweetly to bone,
white bone, and in late spring
too, I remember the bright
young bodies of the boys,

my friends and peers and enemies
till everything breaks down.

## THEN, IF I CEASE DESIRING

Then, if I cease desiring,
you may sing a song
of how young I was.

You may praise famous moments,
all have them, of the churches
I broke into for wine,

not praise, the highways
I travelled drunkenly
in winter, the cars I stole.

You may allow me moments,
not monuments, I being
content. It is little,
but it is little enough.

## BY THE CHURCH WALL

The mocking faces appear in the churchyard,
appear as I curl on the hard ground
trying to sleep—trying to sleep
as the voices call me, asking why
must I always be frightened and dreaming?

I have travelled this road many times,
though not in this place, tired
in the bones and the long blistered feet,
beneath a black mass of flat clouds,
dry in a damned and useless land.

Frogs croak hollowly, the loons cry
their thin bewildered song on a far-off lake,
the wind rises and the wet grass waves;
by the wall of the white rural church
I count a thousand to go to sleep.

But it will not happen. The faces
float before me, bloated and grinning,
succubus and incubus, a child
screams in a house across the road;
I turn and turn in my fear.

There is nothing to hurt me here,
and I know it, but an ancient dread
clenches my belly and fluttering heart,
and in the cold wet grass I count
what may happen and what has.

All the mistakes and desires are here,
old nameless shame for my lies,
and the boy's terrible wish to be good and
not to be alone, not to be alone,
to be loved, and to love.

I remember a letter a friend sent,
trivial and gossiping, quite plain,
of no consequence to him, casually typed
and then signed easily by hand,
All our love, and wish I could say that.

But I lie alone in the shadowed grass,
fond only, incapable of love or truth,
caught in all I have done, afraid
and unable to escape, formulating
one more ruinous way to safety.

from *Black Night Window*

### THE HITCHHIKER

On that black highway,
where are you going?—

it is in Alberta
among the trees

where the road sweeps
left and right

in great concrete arcs
at the famous resort—

there you stood on
the road in the wind,

the cold wind going
through you and you

going through the country
to no end, only

to turn again at one sea
and begin it again,

feeling safe with strangers
in a moving car.

## CRAZY RIEL

Time to write a poem
or something.
Fill up a page.
The creature noise.
Huge massed forces of men
hating each other.
What young men do not know.
To keep quiet,
contemporaneously.
Contempt. The robin diligently
on the lawn sucks up worms,
hopping from one to another.
Youthfully. Sixteen miles
from my boyhood home
the frogs sit in the grassy marsh
that looks like a golf course
by the lake. Green frogs.
Boys catch them for bait or sale.
Or caught them, Time.
To fill up a page.
To fill up a hole.
To make things feel better. Noise.
The noise of the images
that are people I will never understand.
Admire them though I may.
Poundmaker. Big Bear. Wandering Spirit,
those miserable men.
Riel. Crazy Riel. Riel hanged.
Politics must have its way.
The way of noise. To fill up.
The definitions bullets make,
and field guns.

The noise your dying makes,
to which you are the only listener.
The noise the frogs hesitate
to make as the metal hook
breaks through the skin
and slides smoothly into place
in the jaw. The noise
the fish makes caught in the jaw,
which is only an operation
of the body and the element,
which a stone would make
thrown in the same water, thrashing,
not its voice.
The lake is not displaced
with one less jackfish body.
In the slough that looks like a golf course
the family of frogs sings. Metal throats.
The images of death hang upside-down.
Grey music.
It is only the listening for death,
fingering the paraphernalia,
the noise of the men you admire.
And cannot understand.
Knowing little enough about them.
The knowledge waxing.
The wax that paves hell's road,
slippery as the road to heaven.
So that as a man slips
he might as easily slide
into being a saint as destroyer.
In his ears the noise magnifies.
He forgets men.

## RIDE OFF ANY HORIZON

Ride off any horizon
and let the measure fall
where it may —

on the hot wheat,
on the dark yellow fields
of wild mustard, the fields

of bad farmers, on the river,
on the dirty river full
of boys and on the throbbing

powerhouse and the low dam
of cheap cement and rocks
boiling with white water,

and on the cows and their powerful
bulls, the heavy tracks
filling with liquid at the edge

of the narrow prairie
river running steadily away.

*

Ride off any horizon
and let the measure fall
where it may —

among the piles of bones
that dot the prairie

in vision and history
(the buffalo and deer,

dead indians, dead settlers,
the frames of lost houses

left behind in the dust
of the depression,

dry and profound, that
will come again in the land

and in the spirit, the land
shifting and the minds

blown dry and empty —
I have not seen it! except

in pictures and talk —
but there is the fence

covered with dust, laden,
the wrecked house stupidly empty) —

here is a picture for your wallet,
of the beaten farmer and his wife
leaning toward each other —

sadly smiling, and emptied of desire.

*

Ride off any horizon
and let the measure fall
where it may —

off the edge
of the black prairie

as you thought you could fall,
a boy at sunset

not watching the sun
set but watching the black earth,

never-ending they said in school,
round: but you saw it ending,

finished, definite, precise —
visible only miles away.

\*

Ride off any horizon
and let the measure fall
where it may —

on a hot night the town
is in the streets —

the boys and girls
are practising against

each other, the men
talk and eye the girls,

the women talk and
eye each other, the indians
play pool: eye on the ball.

*

Ride off any horizon
and let the measure fall
where it may —

and damn the troops, the horsemen
are wheeling in the sunshine,
the cree, practising

for their deaths: mr poundmaker,
gentle sweet mr big bear,
it is not unfortunately

quite enough to be innocent,
it is not enough merely
not to offend —

at times to be born
is enough, to be
in the way is too much —

some colonel otter, some
major-general middleton will
get you, you —

indian. It is no good to say,
I would rather die
at once than be in that place —

though you love that land more,
you will go where they take you.

*

Ride off any horizon
and let the measure fall —

where it may;
it doesn't have to be

the prairie. It could be
the cold soul of the cities
blown empty by commerce

and desiring commerce
to fill up the emptiness.

The streets are full of people.

It is night, the lights
are on; the wind

blows as far as it may. The streets
are dark and full of people.

Their eyes are fixed as far as
they can see beyond each other —

to the concrete horizon, definite,
tall against the mountains,
stopping vision visibly.

## INDIAN WOMEN

Saturday night
kamsack is
something
to lie about,

the streets full
of indians and
doukhobors,
raw men and

fat women (watch
out for
the women people
said, all the men

do is drink
beer and play
pool but watch
out for those

indian women),
cars
driving up
and down the

main street
from the new
high school

building to
the cn
station and
back

again, paved
road where
the rest were
only oiled

gravel in
the good
old summer

time, in the good
old summertime,
son, when
everybody who

was nobody was
out on the street
with a belly

full talking
to beat
hell and
the heat.

## THE DOUBLE-HEADED SNAKE

Not to lose the feel of the mountains
while still retaining the prairies
is a difficult thing. What's lovely
is whatever makes the adrenalin run;
therefore I count terror and fear among
the greatest beauty. The greatest
beauty is to be alive, forgetting nothing,
although remembrance hurts
like a foolish act, is a foolish act.

Beauty's whatever
makes the adrenalin run. Fear
in the mountains at night-time's
not tenuous, it is not the cold
that makes me shiver, civilized man,
white, I remember
the stories of the Indians,
Sis-i-utl, the double-headed snake.

Beauty's what makes
the adrenalin run. Fear at night
on the level plains, with no horizon
and the stars too bright, wind bitter
even in June, in winter
the snow harsh and blowing,
is what makes me
shiver, not the cold air alone.

And one beauty cancels another. The plains
seem secure and comfortable
at Crow's Nest Pass; in Saskatchewan
the mountains are comforting
to think of; among
the eastwardly diminishing hills
both the flatland and the ridge
seem easy to endure.

As one beauty
cancels another, remembrance
is a foolish act, a double-headed snake
striking in both directions, but I
remember plains and mountains, places
I come from, places I adhere and live in.

## IT WAS ALL THERE

I am now a servant only
of what in my innocence
I had wished to make myself.

Successful, I am unsuccessful; complete,
I am more empty than ever.

These compulsive trips
into the mountains
that frighten me, these runnings away —

what reputation do I have to make?

It was all there, all
the time, I could
sit back quietly now and nothing would change.

I have been too careful for that,
The stuttering boy
is known as the glib

obnoxious insulter, but alone
he still hems, picks up things left-handedly,
and cannot make an order.

**WHAT DO YOU WANT?**

I want a good lover
who will not mistreat me
and suffers indignities willingly;
who is so good in bed
she covers my faults and will claim
the skill's mine, and love me,
and gossip too
to enhance my sexual fame —

what do you want,
what do you want?

I want a good lover
who will cook good meals
and listen respectfully;
shine my shoes, back my lies
with invented statistics at parties;
suffer indignities willingly
and be at my heels—

what do you want,
what do you want?

I want a good lover
who will keep her mouth shut
except for my praise to my face
or loudly behind my back;
who hates my enemies
and willingly suffers indignities—

what do you want,
what do you want?

I want a lover
who suffers indignities.

"It was the Egyptians who first made it an offence against piety to have intercourse in temples . . . . Hardly any nation except the Egyptians and the Greeks have any such scruples, but nearly all consider men and women to be, in this respect, no different from animals, which . . . they constantly see coupling in temples or sacred places . . . ."

Thus Herodotus, who goes on, saying:
Such is the theory, but, in spite of it,
I must continue to disapprove
the practice—giving no reason,

but that we know he is a Greek; and later
says that there are not a great many
wild animals in Egypt. Or, Herodotus, in
this country, despite the fabulous tales

of bears in backyards, heroic
prairie housewives wrist-wrestling cougars,
or cabbies cornering them in downtown Victoria.
And we are no Greeks, disapprove

from spite, in spite. For who would see
the happy young husband lug a swollen prick
into evensong after the seaside picnic,
and have to speculate

on his wife's phosphorous belly, clothed
discreetly in nylon? Or want to step
over the sweaty buttocks
of lovers on the museum's lawn, discovering

the public library's elevator controls
slippery with semen, heaving couples
backing up traffic, mouth to mouth love
in the aquarium, the corny dialogue

of post-orgasm
at political meetings, blunting
the September election's thrust? Not me,
though I remember love on a mountain.

In fair weather or foul
we were at it, clothed
in a mountain, a raincoat.
I am no Greek, or Egyptian either,

but now, in Vancouver's rainy weather,
in spite of it all,
I wear that coat, uptown and down, in fall:
and as for her?—she's in Montreal.

## NO SONG

said the bird
in its attitude

caw

declining
the privilege
of music
or melody

caw

standing
on its tree

caw

fingering
the absolute
wood
beneath

## THE DOG

Lying on my back
on the hot prairie
dreaming of
the nervous sea,

my .22 rifle
by my side, my dog
ranging about and snuffing,
content that I

should do nothing, for
he was a damn fool
of a dog, red and curly,
and always scared

away the crows or gophers
before I could shoot,
dreaming of the sea
and anything to do except

what was at hand
I spent the summers,
never thinking anyone
would love me,

never caring beyond
the delight at making
myself feel sad
and the false tears

tightening my throat
as I worked myself down,
never thinking anyone
could love me, not

as I loved myself—except
that red dog, damn fool
running and barking
away toward the town.

**PUBLIC LIBRARY**

So I sat day after day in the smoking room of the library
some book or paper or magazine on my knee
smoking   half reading
half in a dreamed trance    half listening
to the sounds around me   half looking
at the people around me

the sounds   shuffling of canvas covered feet
rubber soled feet   moccasined feet
newspapers being borrowed   being shaken
rustling like a sea or wind
sea of other peoples' lives
wind a movement of other peoples' air and breathing
books crackling as their backs were broken
the flick/flick of fingertips
and fingernails on the corners of pages
snap of shutting decisively
or accidentally    plump lackadaisically
muted thump of being tossed on low tables
abandoned as too boring
having small type and big ideas or big type and small ideas
magazines slapping against other magazines
heavy glossy pages scraping and sliding against each other
pieces of paper being torn   irritating noise
magnification of a snail's death scream
being stepped on   and the sounds of the people

snores grunts slobbers   sighs
aimless and tuneless humming
toneless and breathless whispering of unknown tunes
noise of the man who sat all day
from nine-thirty in the morning until nine at night
going   aaah aaah   every four seconds
the man who blew his nose noisily between his fingertips
ten times an hour
and snapped the slime off his hand   slap
the asthmatic breathing of another
the man who talked to himself
in a strange sounding language
something slavic or made up
giggling and twittering between the phrases
his laughter rising as the day went on
to a higher and higher more hysterical pitch
until when it seemed he would finally have to collapse
from giggling he suddenly flushed
as if insulted by himself
and screamed in english   the anguish language
Son of a bitch   son of a bitch you
put on his hat and left to go home and make supper
for himself in some grey room

old men snorting in bewildered hurt derision at the newspapers
and trying to suck up the mucus in their noses
without having to show a dirty handkerchief
so strong their pride
feeling passed by   abandoned
left alone by all the other three billion

matches being drawn along plaster walls
scraping like magazine pages
small explosions of wooden matches
cigarettes lustily sucked on
cigarettes thrown on the floor
cigarettes ground out with hate on the floor
revenge against old men's diseases
cancer possibilities   against the all night
long coughing and spitting themselves
and the neighbours' coughing and spitting also

people   in canvas shoes   rubber soles
loggers' boots   years-old oxfords with great cavities
moccasins   thick grey woollen socks knee high
old army issue from two wars at least
baggy cuffless pants   cotton workshirts
flannel plaids sweated in for twenty summers and winters
brassbound army and police suspenders
mismatched doublebreasted fantastically wide lapelled
old pointed blue pinstripe suitcoats
relics of other generations   the wearers outside
all generations   other excitements   dancing
polkas in the northland or on the prairies
to screechy violins and accordions
heavy brown horsey overcoats pulling down their thin shoulders
white beard stubble with tobacco stains
grey beard stubble   white hair
grey hair   trembly hands   rheumy eyes
pale watery eyes   shallow ponds
huge bulging veins popping out from necks and foreheads
glasses with cracked lenses

only here and there the younger ones within twenty years of me
a little neater   the hair still coloured
dull the veins
and breathing and spit a little less obvious
a hint of combs and razor blades
and rarely the well-dressed
tightly-girdle-assed pointy-wire-breasted and well-stroked
young woman would come in and look about
as if she had blundered into the wrong toilet
afraid to walk out again immediately
lest we be too obviously insulted

choosing a chair   trying to look unconcerned
lighting a cigarette   sitting in her stiff brassiere
with all the men who could see far enough staring furtively
at her fat knees   shifting around in their chairs
to ease the strain on the crotches of their greasy pants
as forgotten juices stirred

—when her cigarette was half smoked the woman
girl that is   would butt it in the ashtray   fold
her book   carefully preserving the place
and leave for a safer floor on the building
one where she would not feel those shifty eyes
on her breasts   eyes on her legs
evil male eyes endeavouring to see up her
tight skirts   to see her sweating thighs
to see

and sometimes heavy businessmen
come in and blunder out again
like cardiac bears
but of them
I will not speak for I do not know.

## LADY, LADY

Lady, lady, I cannot lie,
I didn't cut down your cherry tree.

It was another man, in another season,
for the same reason.

I eat the stone and not the flesh,
it is the bare bone of desire I want,

something you would throw a dog,
or me, though I insult by saying so.

God knows it is not said
of your body, that it is like

a bone thrown to a dog,
or that I would throw it away, which

moment to moment I cannot remember
under those baggy clothes you wear—

which, if I love and tell,
I love well.

## SAMUEL HEARNE IN WINTERTIME

1.

In this cold room
I remember the smell of manure
on men's heavy clothes as good,
the smell of horses.

It is a romantic world
to readers of journeys
to the Northern Ocean—

especially if their houses are heated
to some degree, Samuel.

Hearne, your camp must have smelled
like hell whenever you settled down
for a few days of rest and journal-work:

hell smeared with human manure,
hell half-full of raw hides,
hell of sweat, Indians, stale fat,
meat-hell, fear-hell, hell of cold.

2.

One child is back from the doctor's while
the other one wanders about in dirty pants
and I think of Samuel Hearne and the land—

puffy children coughing as I think,
crying, sick-faced,
vomit stirring in grey blankets
from room to room.

It is Christmastime—
the cold flesh shines.
No praise in merely enduring.

3.

Samuel Hearne did more
in the land (like all the rest

full of rocks and hilly country,
many very extensive tracts of land,
tittimeg, pike and barble,

and the islands:
the islands, many
of them abound

as well as the main
land does
with dwarf woods,

chiefly pine
in some parts intermixed
with larch and birch) than endure.

The Indians killed twelve deer.
It was impossible to describe
the intenseness of the cold.

4.

And, Samuel Hearne,
I have almost begun to talk

as if you wanted to be
gallant, as if you went
through that land for a book—

as if you were not SAM, wanting
to know, to do a job.

5.

There was that Eskimo girl
at Bloody Falls, at your feet,

Samuel Hearne, with two spears in her,
you helpless before your helpers,

and she twisted about them like
an eel, dying, never to know.

## THE BIG BEND: BY-PASSED HIGHWAY

1.

It goes on in
the past and
the mystery,

steel rusts in
the river,
the cautioning

signs are down,
there will be
incidents

as even the
attempt fades,
the imperfect

mood denoting
an action, all
men are able

to own,
not yet completed.

2.

Apply the principle
of time to
discover

the fault fades out, the mice
run free, the
wild woman

of the woods
(d'sonoqua)
leaves, rats

inhabit the shacks
of dead men.

3.

We are the masters
of the dead
shale on the roadway,

masters of
that, but
also part

of the embryo,
shadows and
red light:

palingenesia,
the qualitative change
furiously

hanging
over a flowering bush.

4.

The bridges break,
liquid
seeps through the ground,

what is
invented?

5.

Go without
vanity now, momentum
more definite:

water splashes
the rocks, how
to define

an imperfect flower,
no silence in
the forest—who knows

what he remembers
or what he invented?

6.

Time may be counted,
permutating
series of

disintegrations
used against
each other, ours

and the roadway's (the
same thing), sepals,
petals, stamens, pistils,

the same
watery forest, broken
bridges, the same unequal

series of
equal units of
discovery:

you, North America,
remote
in the night,

among the trees
and flowers
from anther
to stigma

unused.

**THE PRIDE**

1.

The image/   the pawnees
in their earth-lodge villages,
the clear image
of teton sioux, wild
fickle people the chronicler says,

the crazy dogs, men
tethered with leather dog-thongs
to a stake, fighting until dead,

image: arikaras
with traded spanish sabre blades
mounted on the long
heavy buffalo lances,
riding the sioux
down, the centaurs, the horsemen
scouring the level plains
in war or hunt
until smallpox got them,
the warriors,

image—of a desolate country,
a long way between fires,
unfound lakes, mirages, cold rocks,
and lone men going through it,
cree with good guns
causing terror in athabaska
among the inhabitants, frightened
stone-age people, "so that
they fled at the mere sight
of a strange smoke miles away."

2.

This western country crammed
with the ghosts of indians,
haunting the coastal stones and shores,
the forested pacific islands,
mountains, hills and plains:

beside the ocean ethlinga,
man in the moon, empties
his bucket, on
a sign from spirit
of the wind ethlinga
empties his bucket, refreshing
the earth, and it rains
on the white cities;

that black joker, broken-
jawed raven, most prominent
among haida and tsimshian tribes
is in the kwakiutl
dance masks too—
it was he who brought fire,
food and water to man,
the trickster;

and thunderbird hilunga,
little thought of
by haida for lack of thunderstorms
in their district, goes
by many names, exquisite disguises
carved in the painted wood,

he is nootka tootooch, the wings
causing thunder and the tongue
or flashing eyes engendering
rabid white lightning,
whose food was whales,

called kwunusela by the kwakiutl,
it was he who laid down the house-logs
for the people at the place
where kwunusela alighted;

in full force and virtue
and terror of the law, eagle—
he is authority, the sun
assumed his form once,
the sun which used to be
a flicker's egg, success-
fully transformed;

and malevolence comes to the land,
the wild woman of the woods—
grinning, she wears
a hummingbird in her hair,
d'sonoqua, the furious one—

they are all ready
to be found, the legends
and the people, or
all their ghosts and memories,
whatever is strong enough
to be remembered.

3.

But what image, bewildered
son of all men
under the hot sun,
do you worship,
what completeness
do you hope to have
from these tales,
a half-understood massiveness, mirage,
in men's minds—what
is your purpose;

with what force
will you proceed
along a line
neither straight nor short,
whose future
you cannot know
or result foretell,
whose meaning is still
obscured as the incidents
occur and accumulate?

4.

The country moves on;
there are orchards in the interior,
the mountain passes
are broken, the foothills
covered with cattle and fences,
and the fading hills covered;

but the plains are bare,
not barren, easy
for me to love their people,
for me to love their people
without selection.

5.

In 1787, the old cree saukamappee, aged 75 or thereabout, speaking then
of things that had happened when he was 16, just a man, told david
thompson about the raids the shoshonis, the snakes, had made on the
westward-reaching peigan, of their war-parties sometimes sent 10 days'
journey to enemy camps, the men all afoot in battle array for the encoun-
ter, crouching behind their giant shields. The peigan armed with guns
drove these snakes out of the plains, the plains where their strength had
been, where they had been settled since living memory (though nothing is
remembered beyond a grandfather's time), to the west of the rockies:

these people moved without rest,
backward and forward with the wind,
the seasons, the game, great herds,
in hunger and abundance—

in summer and in the bloody fall
they gathered on the killing grounds,
fat and shining with fat, amused
with the luxuries of war and death,

relieved from the steam of knowledge,
consoled by the stream of blood
and steam rising from the fresh hides
and tired horses, wheeling in their pride
on the sweating horses, their pride.

6.

Those are all stories;
the pride, the grand poem
of our land, of the earth itself,
will come, welcome, and
sought for, and found,
in a line of running verse,
sweating, our pride;

we seize on
what has happened before,
one line only
will be enough,
a single line
and then the sunlit brilliant image suddenly floods us
with understanding, shocks our
attentions, and all desire
stops, stands alone;

we stand alone,
we are no longer lonely
but have roots,
and the rooted words
recur in the mind, mirror, so that
we dwell on nothing else, in nothing else,
touched, repeating them,
at home freely
at last, in amazement;

"the unyielding phrase
in tune with the epoch,"
the thing made up
of our desires,
not of its words, not only
of them, but of something else
as well, that which we desire
so ardently, that which
will not come when
it is summoned alone,
but grows in us
and idles about and hides
until the moment is due—

the knowledge of
our origins, and where
we are in truth,
whose land this is
and is to be.

7.

The unyielding phrase:
when the moment is due, then
it springs upon us
out of our own mouths,
unconsidered, overwhelming
in its knowledge, complete—

not this handful
of fragments, as the indians
are not composed of
the romantic stories
about them, or of the stories
they tell only, but
still ride the soil
in us, dry bones a part
of the dust in our eyes,
needed and troubling
in the glare, in
our breath, in our
ears, in our mouths,
in our bodies entire, in our minds, until
at last
we become them

in our desires, our desires,
mirages, mirrors, that are theirs, hard-
riding desires, and they
become our true forbears, moulded
by the same wind or rain,
and in this land we
are their people, come
back to life again.

## SOLITAIRE

Then he ran away,
the forest going by him

like a motion picture
and the road slid

beneath his feet
until he stumbled in a ditch

beside a small meadow,
hardly a lawn,

with stiff green grass
tough as barb wire,

around an abandoned
plank shack inhabited

by rats, near a shallow
rocky river in the north

of nowhere, and stayed there
with nightmare

and pack rats and water
and wet chocolate bars and cigarettes

until an engine came
and took him back again.

from *The Cave*

## THE ENGINE AND THE SEA

The locomotive in the city's distance, obscure, misplaced, sounds a child's horn on the flat land leading to the cliff of dark buildings,

the foghorns on the water's edge cry back.

Between the sounds men sit in their houses watching machines inform them in Edison's light. In the marshes, the music of ominous living . . .

a leggy insect runs on that surface, frogs wait, fish, angling birds.

In the cities men wait to be told. They sit between the locomotive and the fish. The flat sea and the prairie that was a sea contain them. Images float before their eyes,

men and women acting,

entertaining, rigorously dancing with fractured minds contorted to a joyless pleasure, time sold from life.

The locomotive hums, the prairies hum. Frogs touch insects with their long tongues, the cannibal fish and the stabbing birds

wait.

Night actions flash before uncountable animal eyes. Mice run. Light rain falls in the night.

The frogs are stilled. Between the engine and the sea, the lights go out. People sleep with mechanical dreams, the sea hums with rain, the locomotive shines black, fish wait under the surface of a pinked pool.

Frogs shiver in the cold. The land waits, black, dreaming. Men lie dry in their beds.

History, history!

Under the closed lids their eyes flick back and forth as they try to follow the frightening shapes of their desires.

## THE WIND

On this last desperate day
when the enchanting devil and the formless hero
embrace, when the wind in our minds
is a maniac, when our flesh is slack
as plastic, melted with desire,

let us see each other entire
and exhausted by each other, turning
about and about to escape,
as we have these months—then leave,
dreaming what we might have been.

## DOUKHOBOR

When you die and your weathery corpse
lies on the chipped kitchen table,

the wind blowing the wood of your house
painted in shades of blue, farmer

out from Russia as the century turned,
died, and lay at the feet of the wars,

who will ever be able to say for you
what you thought at the sight of the Czar's horsemen

riding with whips among you, the sight
of the rifles burning on bonfires,
in
the long sea-voyage, strange customs endured,
officials changing your name

into the strange script that covered the stores,
the polite brown men who spoke no language

you understood and helped you
free your team from Saskatchewan winter mud,
river
who will be able to say for you
just what you thought as the villages marched

naked to Eden and the English
went to war and came back again

with their funny ways, proud
to speak of killing each other, you, whose mind

refused the slaughter, refused the blood,
you who will lie in your house, stiff as winter,

dumb as an ox, unable to love,
while your women sob and offer the visitors tea?

- note changes from _The Cave_, 1970

## THE PRAIRIE

One compiles, piles, plies
these masses of words, verbs,
massifs, mastiffs barking meaning,
dried chips
of buffalo dung, excreta from beasts

the prairie fed, foddered,
food for generations: men roaming
as beasts seen through dips
in history, fostered by legend,
invented remembrance. Scenes shake,

the words do not suffice. One bred
on the same earth wishes himself
something different, the other's
twin, impossible thing, twining
both memories, a double meaning,

but cannot be—never
to be at ease, but always migrating
from city to city
seeking some almost seen
god or food or earth or word.

**BEFORE SLEEP**

Until you lie down in the dark again
to see with nightmare this depressed slant
of winter light   a cold sick yellow
clouded   morose   that lies on your eyes

before you sleep   ideas locked
firmly in place   before you sleep
to wake and wash the sleep from your face

with cold water   cupped in your hands
that have curled in nightmare
half the night long   until the fear
clings to the back of your mind   only forgotten

until you lie down in the dark again to see
the white faces floating and the mouths that say
urgently   Listen to me   Listen only to me

the familiar faces like fathers turning
just out of sight of the dreaming eyes   names
almost remembered   mothers of hatred and fear
and cousins to murder   strangers seeking

you for themselves   Remember how real
your waking life seemed   until you lay down
in the dark and pulled
a sheet to your head

## REVENGE

He thought of the hammer.
He got up, holding his arm
as if it were already broken.

He went downstairs again.
Coming into the kitchen
he held up his arm before his eyes,

gloating, already triumphant.
They'll feel sorry for me,
they'll feel sorry for me.

He let go of the arm, got
a plain glass out of the cupboard,
filled it with cold tapwater.

He drank, he regarded his arm,
he considered the hammer.
Exultation strengthened in him.

## BY THE GREY ATLANTIC

Among the green trees of Vancouver
it was being in a dream,
a dream of life, remembered,
the future recalled; dream men,
dream women, walking.

Here by the grey Atlantic
it is being a dream
of death remembered,
the past recalled; dead men
and dead women, talking.

## GOD BLESS YOU

What I like is this Atlantic.
Guns practise outside my window.

But, this ocean: here men have drowned.
You can see it in the grey waves.

Eyes roll in the troughs, hands reach.
White flesh drapes the actual weeds.

This is water men die, not swim, in.
God bless you, if you go in a bathing suit

to hell.

## REMEMBERING CHRISTOPHER SMART

Being a small person bound
in a small circle, I think
of large things, obscurely . . . .

But what is so obscure
as I am, my brothers? I can discern
the motives that impel me,
not fight them. Wearing clothes
annoys me but every morning
I get up and pull my underwear on.

When I think of my cat Boots,
grey as dawn but white-legged,
who took over the whole chesterfield
from my fat father who'd won a military medal
in the first world war,
and lay there insolently stretched out,
the whole body yawning as cats do,
I see that even amoebas can rule the world,
and who says the justice would be less?

No. When I consider a small person
such as myself, dreaming of women,
those legs once again and that warmness,
just to lie there, to lie,
I see that we all make the world what we want.
Our disappointment lies in the world as it is.

*no changes from The Cave, 1970*

## AMERICA

Even the dissident ones speak
as members of an Empire, residents
of the centre of the earth. Power
extends from their words
to all the continents and their modesty
is liable for millions. How must it be
to be caught in the Empire, to have
everything you do matter? Even
treason is imperial; the scornful
self-abuse comes from inside the boundaries
of the possible. Outside the borders of royalty
the barbarians wait in fear,
finding it hard to know which prince
to believe; trade-goods comfort them,
gadgets of little worth, cars, television,
refrigerators, for which they give iron,
copper, uranium, gold, trees, and water,
worth of all sorts for the things
citizens of Empire take as their due.

In the Empire power speaks from the poorest
and culture flourishes. Outside the boundaries
the barbarians imitate styles and send their sons,
the talented hirelings, to learn and to stay;
the sons of their sons will be princes too,
in the Estate where even the unhappy
carry an aura of worldly power; and the lords
of power send out directives
for the rest of the world to obey. If they live
in the Empire, it matters what they say.

## ALCAZAR *(Vancouver tavern of lowlife)*

I think I've seen you somewhere,
said the girl in the pub, sitting
at the next table. We joined her,
but could not think where
we might have been together.

At the same table, the fat woman
(happy or sad) said, I wish
I was a bird, I'd take my suitcase
in my beak and fly away
to Copenhagen. Copenhagen?

But that girl in the pub: she was plump,
not smart. She sat
with her husband, married
after a 9-day knowledge of him,
English sailor, ship-jumper.

I'm flying to Copenhagen,
the fat woman said; her suitcase
was not in her beak. The girl and I
could not think where we might have been
together. The beer mounted in us.

The fat woman dreamed. The sailor
complained of the beer and the cigarettes here;
the girl spoke of her marriage
and husband. It would be all right, she said,
if he wouldn't burn me with cigarettes.

*change from The Cave, 1970*

87

DREAM

The luxurious trembling sea, winding atmosphere of thick death and life,
egg-filled, swarming and empty,

rides on unknown rock and infested slabs of slime epochs deep in flesh
that has no memories,

no interest except to live, survive, shambling through cold currents, only
occasionally breaking the shining opaque lid of the wet universe,

a touch of animal foam on the surface among the few floating twigs that
drift away from the deserted earth . . . .

And the red and brown vine-tangled land is empty except for armoured
insects lugging their invaluable trophies back and forth,

dry matted grass feet deep whipped in the wind, rotten fallen trees, crisp
shards of leaves,

shifting deserts of sand and bare plains strewn with rocks like ankle bones
stretching across the sterile continents, dust in the stark air,

no movement except that of ants and beetles and the great swaying
wooden vegetables, dead . . . .

The sea moves nervously, through it strange beasts search for food,
unthinkingly constant in their paths,

the earth rustles dryly and in the bright sky the stars continue to shine,

and the great galaxial wheel rolls smoothly in its unhuman silence that
contains all sounds . . . .

## THE APPARITION

An apparition slackwitted
   with disaster climbed
into the bus today,
   red hair, hunchbacked,
Richard the Third's movie face,
   thin white propped legs,
a brown coat, speckled
   white and brown dishcover
hat, flat, something
   to enfold a dish of cold potatoes—

her discontent
   hangs in the air,
a thick curdled yellow floating
   in the dissatisfied air
as she has a friendly
   little talk with the driver,
pout wrinkling the long chin,
   handsome face obscurely handsome,
very definite, set,
   set in eccentricity, uncalculated
finally, finally necessary,
   an abandoned pasture—

posture (the mind's stutter
   as it avoids what has happened
and tries to invent concern
   beyond what is important)—

life made mad by metabolism
   of the shoulder-blades and legs,
no distortion innate
   in the mind but that forced on it
by the world and the unslavelike body.

**THE FAT MAN**

1.

A fat man holding flowers regards the traffic light
above him, hand made fist around
the flowers and the paper that wraps their stems, hand
balancing on the abrupt ridge of his stomach,
a shelf. The hand, furthest forward in space,
followed then by his face placed back
even more, necklessly leaning on the sloping shoulders
above a spindle-chest:
this hand makes a straight line passing
through the blooms of the flowers,
through the fat man's open black mouth, by the back of his head
to the glass light of the traffic signal.

He regards the glare of the signal, the light it gives, not
the thing itself. Light from it
slants down his forehead, bounces over the eyebrows'
projecting spur of bone, leaving the sockets themselves
dark. He is a fat and male Orphan Annie
with black eyes. Light divides along his nose and dribbles
off his chin. Led down that trail, it scatters
amongst the petals of the flowers and then
diffuses in diluted patches on his hand.

Light rain begins to fall. A small wind drives.
At night the ocean wind this time of year
brings rain. I turn my face and let
the little water sting me. The fat man
has not moved. He still observes
the traffic-signal's glow. He will not let it
get away.
       He moves his hat
over the flowers, a gesture. Water
spatters off his half-bald head. A gesture;
he does not need to do that. The flowers do not
need protection from the rain; he does.

He has no petals; he is more than half-bald.
Oh, hair covers half his skull
but that hair is thin; it streams
about his ears. His hair is cut
long at the sides: pretence of hairiness;
he suspects that the office boys call him
skinhead or bonehead, as he would have done
if things were different or reversed.

2.

Perhaps the girls
call him bonehead too,
behind his back
or around corners,
out of the sides
of their lovely mouths;
he was almost sure
that he might have heard
one of those girls
saying bonehead about him
to another, the big one,
the big girl saying.

He is taking the flowers
home to his wife
but now his hair
is wet and it hangs
down like a dog's,
obeying the rain
and the slanting wind;
he holds his head back
to catch the light,
he does not want
to lose a second; he
has paid for time.

The rain makes even me
sniff and as for him
it is now running down
both sides of his nose
in the red light.
The rain drops spatter
on the top of his head,
microcosmic atomics.
He does not uncover
the flowers, the brim
of his hat still covers
the grasping hand. His arm
ends at the shirtcuff.
The hand is obscured.

If he does that enough
it will make him sick.
He is bald and fat and aging
and that is enough.
He will catch pneumonia
or even TB,               *T.B., in The Cave*
and at the office they
will say that that was right
because he is a tuber,
a sweet potato. He knows
the jokes they make.

And he would die
from tuberculosis
or even if he survived
he would lie for years
in a white sanatorium,
antiseptic, and cough
phlegm spotted with blood
and spit phlegm spotted
with red red blood
into his handkerchief
or into some old
wadded-up bits
of toilet paper.

He would have to keep
a roll on the table
beside his bed;
there could never be
handkerchiefs enough
and everyone would see
the handy toilet paper
and know what it was for,
and on the white enamelled
table there would be
a water glass with two or three
small flowers in it.
He would grow sick of their look
and smell. He hates flowers.

The nurse would put new blooms
into the glass each week
and there would be brown stains
around the middle of the glass
as the dirty water she forgot
evaporated. And the pretty nurse          no period, no A in   The Cave
would watch him spitting phlegm
spotted with red red blood
into his little piece
of wadded-up toilet paper and she
would feel disgusted—
how much easier life would be
if only women were ugly!

But perhaps he will just catch a cold.
Nothing has happened yet.
Even the worst of dreams
sometimes fails to come true.
At least he will catch a cold;
it will make him miserable
all winter and he
will have to wipe his nose
in the middle of composing letters
into the dictaphone, or blow.
He will be forced to sniff
during the prayers in church,
as if he disapproved.

3.

He should let the rain fall on the flowers equally
with his head so that they will last long enough
to ornament his coffin when he dies. Red flowers
will ornament his coffin when he dies
while his wife and the mourners twirl round him.

The office boys and the girls from the office
will stand stiff in the pews to watch
the coffin covered with red light thrown
from the stained glass of the church,
windows showing the martyrdoms of saints.

They will not see his face because his head
will be turned to the altar, his feet
turned toward them; his stomach will be in the way.
Perhaps the people in charge or his wife
will forget to buy him new shoes for the service.

His feet will be wearing his best
pair of black shoes, worn on the bottoms:
but they will all forget he was bald,
he will have flowers instead of hair,
and no one will ever again see his face.

4.

No, they won't forget.
Salesmen will come into the office
and ask if so-and-so is in,
his own dead name. The secretaries will say,
Dead Name? I don't remember him . . . .
Oh yes, the bald one, he isn't here anymore,
I think he left or something . . . .

5.

The traffic light turned green.
It cast its night-time vegetative glow
onto the fat man's raised face, changing it
into a puffed-up lime. He brought
down his head. He was dead already.
Green light glinted off the whites of his eyes,    "white" in The Cave
exposed now. His mouth closed.
Bald man. Fat man. He stepped off the edge
of the sidewalk as off
the roof of the world's tallest building.
Darkness and rain gathered about him
as he walked down the tunnelling street,
a tarpaper blob retreating with flowers, home
to sleep and dreams and his apple-pie wife.

## THE CAVE

The stars are your deathbed.
You rest from the cave
to Pluto or whatever dark planets
lie beyond. No ideas trap you.

In the unobstructed sunlight miles high
the Earth is beautiful as a postcard.
Sinai looks as the map says it should,
and people are too small to be observed.

In Africa there are no trees to see.
It is a map world.
The sunlight is brilliant
as a two-carat diamond on a girl's hand.

The girl is young, visible to your mind,
growing older. Beyond Pluto
and the darkest planets, children surround her.

The diamond glows on her finger
like a worm. The stars, the stars
shine like one-carat diamonds. Beyond
Pluto and the darkest planets the stars shine.

The diamonds shine in wormy rings
on fingers, in coffins of unobstructed space.
The flesh circles the bone in strips
in the coffin as the ring circled flesh.

The two-carat sun hangs loosely,
just restraining the Earth. Beyond the planets,
beyond the dark coffin, beyond the ring of stars,
your bed is in the shining, tree-lit cave.

**THE FLOWER**

I am too tense,
decline to dance
verbally. The flower
is not in its colour,
but in the seed.

from *Lies*

## AND THE DEAD ROSE UP FROM THE WATER

Coming alive at the age of thirty,
refusing a few years
to abandon my despair,
and the dead rose up from the water,
their heads buoys in front of my love;
I tried to kiss them alone
but the water moved their pale fleshy faces.

This year ten million Bengalis
met old enemies—exile
and cholera, bullets, knives. This year
corpses returned from the moon. Traitors
to humans flourished.

Children . . . children, what are you doing?
I despair of *you.*
I don't care if you kill yourselves, but
why kill me? I have only come alive
for a moment; and I wish I were dead,
or kissing the ocean's lovers,
brown foam on their opened eyes.

## THE HERO AROUND ME

Water submissive and cool, the abundant sun
hot on my white back, day
of quiet pleasures, air humming
a steady soothing tune through the long hours,
ghosts slowly drifting past,
heads like broad arrows, hair coiled
about faces. Time is sliding away . . . .

I have desired many
but I wonder if I have loved one?—
remembering the cruel amusement and pleasure
of a youth called hard-hearted,
joy in a tearful eye and a frantic manner,
dismissive joy, and the day
humming and sliding away . . . .

Once heroes marched through my mind
in solid ranks, the deeds
shaped pointedly, and I knew
I could never be one of them,
though I desired it, wished for one sharp moment
in my life—thinking
of the hero as man in combat only . . . .

The day came, but not as war.
Fields of grain around me were crystal,
the sky polished, endless gold and blue,
and in the still heat a meadowlark
twisted its sculptured tune around me
once, quickly, a deft feat of superior magic,
and all time stopped, world without end,
and I was as a tree is, loathing nothing.

**THE SKY**

Never knowing how we got there
one day we woke and saw the sky,
limitless, serene, capable
of black cloud and lightning,
the land limitless, yellow
with grain in summertime,
light green in spring, stretching
to the edge of the world
but never ending; and it made us
want to go.
   We travelled westward,
a little further every time,
venturing the hills, venturing
the spirit-inhabited mountains,
the quick down-slope, viewing at last
the sea and the sea-city.

The city was wonderful, huge;
we never heard that there were no birds.

How small all our own cities seemed,
so tiny, one street only, limited,
lacking the towers, the veritable ocean,
strange trees.
   Later we woke,
and saw the sky, crammed by mountains
as we were, open only to the sea,
westward; and could not swim.

**WHITE LIES**

The winter shines, I think.
But it's summer now and I'm not home.
The sky is the colour of a pike's belly,
the air stinks. It is pretending
to be about to rain. The atmosphere
is heavy, is glue. Glum glue.

I seem to remember those winters.
The hard-surfaced snow
would have stretched tightly
over the low hills, vast pearls
glowing in the night of five o'clock,
white lies.

Bright cars cautious on the roads,
the grey skeleton trees, occasional greens,
rarely a rabbit's convulsive flash,
black birds sitting on telephone wires,
waiting, waiting.

I haven't been home for years.

## SLOW SPRING

Lime-green pants and a red polka-dot handkerchief,
    hanging-on-a-line.
      The trees are sallow, trying
          to pretend to be alive. Touch them
And your fingers
Will stick together
    like people on a slow train.
    Their eyes follow you everywhere, yellow and grey.

The air is colder than your dreams could be.
The carved boulder in your shoe
    is only a pebble,
        and small.
In the wind spider webs sway.
This is Spring, soft ashes falling to the ground.

## OF TIME

*i*

false hope.
little is done.
the seed
in the gift,

in the gift
of time,

is a little,

is done.

false hope.
the seed
of time,

the seed
is a little.

but time
is the gift, the

tentative movement.

*ii*

false hope
in the gift.
in the gift

is a little.
in the gift,
false hope.

in the gift
is a little
tentative
movement,

a little.


but the seed
of time
is done.

*iii*

but time
is done.

the seed
of time,
tentative
movement,
is done.

false hope.

but tentative

movement

is a little.
the seed
is a little

false hope
in the gift.

*iv*

ten-
tative,
the seed.

the seed,
false hope,
is a little.

false hope
is done
of time.

of time
but movement
is done.
the seed,

the seed
alone
is done.

## THE POOL

1.

And in his dreams he came once to a clear sunken pool
in the middle of the forest of pines, water
from an older continent, floored
by long green grasses
wavering on their sides through the refraction.
The pool itself lay calmly, calmly surrounded
by a perfect circle of grey stone ledge.
Hot resin of the pines flavoured the air.

How does anyone ever know
how he has got where he is? The silver water
lay in a circular clearing. No fish
swam in it. The trees stood up
straightly to the sky.

Magic, magic. He stood
with his arms stiff by his sides and his head bent,
watching his reflection on the surface of the pool.

Stillness about him was absolute. For hours
there had been no sound
but that of his body walking among the pines,
going farther and farther away from the world.
As he moved the forest expanded.

His mind slid off objects.
He tried to look at himself in the pool,
squinting, but only a squinting figure peered back.
He could not make out its eyes.

How had he got where he was? He remembered
walking
and the sound of walking
in the past,
then an effortless drifting, his body
pulled forward toward the pool,
surer with each step.

2.

It was dark and he lay down to sleep.
As he slept he dreamed.

He dreamed that he rose in the night,
turning his back on the silver
stone-encased water
                    with never a look at it, eyes averted,
leaving the clearing in the pines.
Cool air of midnight diminished the resinous odour.
The scent was clean.

Nothing impeded as he left the circle.
Silently he walked through the shrinking forest.
The night softened the needles beneath his feet.

From the forest's edge he emerged into brilliant light.
Red buildings stood against the sky.
Beams probed for raiders, a mass of humans ran like a herd,
the sound of desperate breathing,
sirens and lights rushed towards him, machines
screamed . . . .

3.

He woke up, sweating and cramped,
and said, I won't wake up,
and woke up.

**COMPANY**

1.

It is a man.

It sits in the public library
coveting the women it fears.

They sense it has been without a woman a long time
and they loathe it.

They smell the worst kind of celibacy on it,
involuntary.

There is a rancidness, a smell of having given up,
of having been given up on:
if no one cares then no one will care.

It is not the worn jeans
or the shirt seeming to have been on one day too long
no matter how newly washed;
it is not the fingernails, cut or uncut, dirty or clean,
or the yellow tobacco smear along the side of the finger,
or the hair, combed or uncombed;
it is not a matter of fixing the teeth,
nothing to do with blackheads
or with the awkward shape or even with money:
women are generous when they are able to be.

It is the smell of hopelessness,
it is fear's emanation, that ulcerates the stomach.
Women edge away from it, feeling something unhuman,
the wrong condition of longing, the wrong character of need,
the long time waiting.

2.

It loves company and company is disgusted by it;
company enjoys being disgusted by it;
it enjoys disgusting company.

It thinks that it likes to act
as company expects it to act:
cadging, begging, groping,
insolent subservience,
arrogant whining.

In the nape of its neck it feels
that it knows all about people,
what they think or expect:
but they know all about it. They are willing
to enjoy their disgust, to be amused,
so long as the price is not too high.
When the price is too high
they will cease to be amused.

Then it will not have company.
It will have to go somewhere else.

The same things will occur in another place.
Things will always occur.
And back again. The same rhythms.
But shorter
durations. The time
always gets shorter. Until
in a rush at last there is no time.
At all.

3.

It will sit sour in seventy-five cent
or free Salvation Army and welfare barracks
and tell the other bums what it might have been
or done
and listen to what they might have been or done—
moving from cot to cot,
and all of the beds in all of the cities the same.

4.

Sky blue.
Phony-looking fluffy white postcard clouds
lumping slowly along in the hot sky.

Beach with grass, washed-up logs, sand.
Then mixed sand and shells and pebbles,
and dark green-black vegetable sludge from the sea.

Then pebbles and sludge and shells,
then stones and shells,
then yellowish foam flecked with white,
then small fat lazy rolls of water
with sticks floating on it.

Fueling stations for boats anchored in the water,
a few power boats, a few sail boats,
the ocean.

And impossible miles across there are the islands of the Pacific,
imagined decorations in a romantic atlas, alien histories,
Polynesia, Melanesia, Micronesia . . . an atlas
full of life—

Even if the cannibals dance,
anywhere but here where people know it . . . .

5.

It doubles over,
takes off its shoes and socks.

It sits down on the sand,
hands propped behind it,
legs stuck stiffly out;
it feels a trace of shame.

It is pale.
There is dirt between its toes and around the nails.
It digs its feet into the sand to cover them.

The sun is hot.
Gulls squawk.

There are girls and women on the beach and in the water.
It tries not to look at the flesh.

6.

Memories drift past;
they cannot be grasped.

To remember without lying is difficult.
With friends, drinking beer, there is a set of rules,
a code of telling—
                        that covers the errors,
the cowardices and stupidities,
turning them into weak amusing virtues,
anecdotes in which no one really wins or loses.

7.

When there are no friends
at least there must be companions occasionally.

It would be too much
to sit in a room alone all of the time
or on the edge of a cot in a noisy room.

8.

Remembering seems like a slow train now,
that goes on its tracks.

To ride is to go where the train goes,
or the way the train goes,
though not always all the way.

Not always?
Never.

9.

It takes its feet out of the sand.
It stands up and walks to the edge of the ocean.

Wavelets cover its feet and touch its ankles at times.
The water is cool and pleasant.

It walks back to where it had been
and stands looking at its feet.

It has forgotten the girls and the women on the beach,
the flesh.
When its feet are dry it will put on its socks and shoes
and walk off the beach
with its head down
and cross the bridge to the centre of the city
to the smoking room of the public library.

10.

Perhaps something will happen.
Perhaps something good will happen.

Perhaps it will meet someone it knows
or someone who knows it.

Him.

They would talk together about the past.
They would agree with each other.
They would drink beer and smoke and talk confidently
about women
until closing time.

Then they would part,
not contradicting each other.

*no changes*

## OF MY OWN FLESH

Hard crystals there are hard crystals inside them
in their bellies and their hands
curl up when they talk to you their eyes narrow
as if the sun were burning into them
and they smile

They smile their lips
draw back stiffly from the pale enamelled teeth the pain
cramping the cheek muscles is shown
in the grooves cut in their faces in
the eyebrows

They wish they would turn to stone they hate
to have feeling they hate you
for feeling it is not right they think
for me to be careful not to hurt
because I want to hurt

In the ball of my clenched hand talons are growing
it is the palm of my own flesh they enter
they ought to be furrowing yours
it is your skin that should be ripped
your blood flowing

Hard crystals I have hard crystals in my belly
claws are growing where my nails were
my heels are round stones to grind you
my muscles bunch to kill you
to cut you to see blood

I am becoming a statue
here in the glare of my own dead eyes
I am becoming a statue

## SHE

She starts to grow tears, chemical beast
shut in a dark room with the walls closing
behind her eyelids, all touches hateful,
the white sweep of clean snow death to her,
the grey naked trees death to her.

Her face swells. Tears
slide like glycerine down the round cheeks
and shimmer on her chin. No motion
escapes her face; sadness gathers
in her bones; her fingers curl, an ulcer
pins her down, rotting in her body.

The quiet shadows on the screen
dance, gesticulate, the news comes on and goes,
cars are sold, women sing and smile,
but she does not. Still the tears
run down without a sound. She curls
on her couch; she moves a bit, moves heavily,
as if she had forgotten how.

She moves. The snow shines through the window,
a phosphorescent sea, gleaming;
the etched ghosts of the night sway slightly.

The grass is dead. In spring
it will not be the same, the trees
with their sticky shiny leaves will only be
in costume, mocking, the fresh air
will lie; animals stretching in their skins
stretch to die. But she moves.

She moves. Her shoulders ache. She feels
the harnesses she lives in, she feels
the jelly on her skeleton, she feels the tears
upon her face and dries them with her hands,
touches her hair, sits up and tries to smile.

It is a brave attempt, saying: See how brave I am!
Her breasts hang heavy on her, and the room is dark.

*no changes*

**DREAM**

Bees won't fly when it's this cold;
sixty degrees is what they need.

Wings freeze. A hundred miles beyond
the white frontier the European honey bee

frightens the natives. They know it;
it moves ahead. Wings freeze, though.

In winter one Indian
moves slowly through the snow,
hoping for sweetness, a taste.


**DREAM**

The lone figure leans in the snow.
A rifle is stuck beside him:
one hand is on it.

He waits an approaching figure.
He will decide, when it comes,
to kill or to run.

It is the white centre of the world
his reason squats in.

## WHY DO YOU HATE ME?

So you live of the sea;
and I am the dry acrid land.

You have the sweet fish swimming
and dull mannerly grain grows in me.

Your blood shines in curving darts;
I grow in calculated rows.

So I say I love you,
and you say, Why do you hate me?

I speak in a foreign language.
You don't know what I say.


## EVERYWHERE I GO

What are people talking about. Everywhere I go they whisper.

They stick their eyes at me, right at the base of the breastbone, when I'm not looking.

The breastbone is flat, pointed like a dagger to the top of my stomach.

O, my stomach, my stomach . . . when the knife rips you open it will find coffee and four strips of bacon, pieces of chewed beard and a handwritten note saying I have left town forever again.

## HARRY, 1967

Old Harry just sits on the porch all day staring at himself and not seeing a damn thing.

Or to tell the truth he doesn't even sit on the porch. His house hasn't got a porch.

Or to tell the truth Harry hasn't got a house.

Harry lives in a ten-dollar-a-week light-housekeeping room and thinks of himself sitting on the porch of a house he never had.

Harry has become very familiar with oatmeal and macaroni in his old age. He is thirty-six, born in 1931.

Born after the First World War, born after the twenties, born just in time to barely remember a small portion of the Depression, born too young to fight in the Second World War, to remember details really well.

Harry is five foot seven and a half, Harry weighs one hundred and thirty pounds, Harry has dandruff, Harry has bad teeth and no prospect of ever getting them fixed, Harry wears glasses, Harry quit school at sixteen before he finished Grade Nine to get in on the big money.

Harry looks like he's had TB all his life but Harry hasn't, Harry has nothing and looks like getting less.

But Harry sits on that porch all day feeling the sunlight almost and not seeing a damn thing. It's been a lousy life and it's only just half over.

Harry is thirty-six and he doesn't even dream about women anymore. Harry knows he'll never touch a woman again.

So what's the use of thinking about it.

But Harry used to see things.

Harry went to Ethiopia and was a general in a revolution.

And he killed the emperor with his own hand.

And his gallant tribesmen swept down upon the lines of khaki machine-gunmen and sabred every one of them.

Harry was nicked by a fragment of shell that left an inch-long cut like one a knife would make on his forearm.

And Harry had no expression on his face when he removed the cigarette from his mouth and used its burning tip to cauterize the wound while fat newspapermen gasped in admiration as the faint smell of toasted flesh reached them.

And the movie cameras whirred.

And Harry waved his sword and ordered his cavalry to charge and all around the world movie audiences watching the Movietone News gasped as Harry slaughtered the old Emperor himself and his admiring tribesmen crowned Harry king and Harry . . . .

Harry always thought the word was calvary not cavalry, legacy of a short time at Sunday School in the damp cloakroom of a prairie United Church.

That was a long time ago to Harry and he has a long time to go.

And Harry doesn't see anymore.

He doesn't know that it's useless to see things that can never happen, he doesn't know that for him dreaming is just a lie now, that seeing things is no good for him, too late: that isn't why Harry doesn't see.

Harry just can't anymore, that's all.

## QUOTATIONS

*It is our duty*

It is our duty to proceed
from what is known to that
which is not.
          The century began
with barbarians dominant; the twisted smile
and the curious sad dishonest eyes
formed a cultural frontier. Stress
the monstrous nature of the act of blood,
the oldest contract.
          I was parched,
my throat burned, and I said:
This is the taste of death.

Snakes and a boy born without arms,
the irrational terrors of shaman and seer,
miserable beautification
built great empires,
          the continents falling away,
a huge tangle of forests
infested by men with rifles.

Someone always foresaw the future accurately.
The most dangerous of foes was an age of Empires,
legacies of mutual hatreds, memory
without an experience. There is nothing
more bitter.
          I, even I, must die sometime
in the caves and caverns of the dark and gloomy earth.

We only came to dream.
It is not true, it is not true—
that we came to live on the earth.

*The first step toward ruin*

Without faltering that first step toward ruin . . . .
Nightly serenaded with drunken songs . . . .

The diseased taste of the people wore a tippet of human scalps.

A sad honesty, habitable and trespassable,
had been surrendered. The next adaptation glowed smokily.

The sacrificial animal was fertility.


*Through fear of novelty*

Through fear of novelty as well as expense
no love or justice is worshipped,
reaches its heights in these years.

Death is everywhere in the temples, idol towers,
cement for building manufactured from blood.
Rings adorn cold fingers.

In the very beginning the savage conqueror
has heard everything and does not mind,
does not listen,
just as an old man is loathe to sing—

There is a way of dying on cue. Turn out of the way
of him who bears in his hands
a terrifying creature, half beast, half divine.

*Among so many memories*

Most of those who came from the north,
from the oceans and the mountain ranges,
killed without compunction while ladies in night-linen
crooned songs to their husbands. Sham heroes
are popular.
                    Amid so many memories of blood and outrage,
despite every novelty, draw back the veil
that is thinly spread over the skeleton,
that Tower of Silence.


*To have been little*

Poor, sullen, superstitious, with unwashed faces,
speaking goblin language, regarding the ruled
as a flock or a herd to be tended, the inhabitants
were almost impenetrable.
                    The pious
perplexed their butchers by dancing,
contemptible in the sight of all.

From men and beasts creating fantastic republics
many dangers ascended;
cannibals persisted obstinately.

The bloody and destructive ceremonies
produced a small grammar; the more active conspirators
accepted the Ideal arrayed in the Actual.

Take your sleep in a swine-sty;
there seems to have been little to conquer.
The supple genius closed in disaster.
Intelligence ended.
                    The use of the sword
left no resentment behind it.
                                        Do not forget.

*They stood upright*

They stood upright in their ranks,
corpse supporting corpse; the trite
touched with the strange, incapable
of defending her own frontiers.

The mass moved of itself, the trail
splashed with blood in a zigzag course,
product of an *age*, product
of *historical forces*.

Ruin came from great men. Awe
and mutual suffering
were in those dead minds,
imitative and contagious,
absolute impotence at the core.

*Cities die*

Cities die just like men. There is no scorn more profound
than that of the use of machines. Harried and disunited,
better a city ruined than a city lost. It cannot be helped.

A mad state cannot long stand. Emotional parasites never wilt,
submitting to fortune, accident, contingency, charms
to measure time. Such methods look like chance.

Unde malum et qua in re? In process of time many returned
like dogs to their vomit to be the quest of the time,
but we remained sunk in greed and sloth and sensuality.

*Disease*

Disease has seized the treasury; the precious
object has been lost. I have decided
to go into the Camp of my Enemies
and be eaten by their dogs.

Bands of ecstatic holy men. Venomous involutions
spreading havoc. Slow conversion. Stuffed baboons
nagging the big gleaming birds with ornaments. The flimsy
and fraudulent republic reigns.

The stupider one is
the clearer one sees: a remote race
is kept for meat, barbarian people,
bad faces. A brighter wall has finally crumbled.

*You don't need to live*

Profitable crusades incapable of wanting to know the truth
conquer a country, its greatest vigour and renown, crazy
about miracles, about something more than passing trifles.
The Exterminating Angel governs the tenure of the throne.

What is not given to man cannot be vouched for
by human minds, those secure dependencies, devotees
of the moon, of the purged carnival, of food in plenty.

An alphabet in a turquoise mine is no evidence
like that of the blood of the freshly murdered young;
hunting invaders over a lifeless world
draws no dead up.
                    Ruin and fire and flood,
the whole sensible appearance of things
in an ocular illusion to con the leading beasts
into thinking the world of the poor
still has fat at the roots of its heart.

The sole arbiter of life and death is the sedimentary plain,
the crystalline shield, full moon, hunter's moon, bomber's moon,
the cold mountain-side.

You don't have to live if you have no dreams.
Amen. Amen.

## IN THE CRAMMED WORLD

1.

Tired, unsure, fearing war, in the crammed world surrounded,
leafless trees rising from the cold ground, a man
stoops as the grey slatted sky presses down,
unwilling to think of the possible facts of a future day.

Nights are spent among the seductive beasts, smiling and calling,
each earnest as a rock. Dreams rise and waver, slipslide,
echoing the stonegreen undersea they represent themselves as,
filled with weeds, cutting reefs, long strips of slit muscle
contracting silently. Teeth are scattered on the cool sand, not shells.

This is the region of the bleak weasel, ribby, at the shore. He sneaks
through the blind landscape sniffing blood among the useless vegetables;
wind sprays the tall grass stalks with poisons from the yellow air;
somewhere there a weak face smiles carefully.

Under water or above not success nor failure inhabits the dreams;
only fear, too near to be unwelcome always. The mind
scares itself with spectres more friendly than the world of smoke:
one may escape from them, not from concrete and jails.

2.

A man starved of something he will not admit admires his skinniness,
in sorrow; each exposed bone is an honourable medal. He says, Comfort
my sad eyes. It is pleasure I want from your proffered breast,
not that thin gruelly milk that drips from the nipple.
Accept my suffering, which is all I have made of my life,
which is all the love I want to offer you.

3.

Painful man, your hurt lasts longer than a movie;
it will not amuse a woman or the future for so long. New turns
must be invented every day. And newer tricks. So dream;
    dream of success,
and hope, though hope for what you cannot guess, but when you slide
with your eyes closed into the universe you invented viciously,
do not complain that the wrong doors open wide, open, wait,
then close behind you,
and some friendly animal long thought of greets you and grows fat
lapping your red gore.